China's Nationalist Policies Obscuring Reality in Tibet

Kevin Kieswetter

Preface

In 2014, I wrote "Chariots of Fire: A Tibetan Historical Perspective" as an introduction for those interested in the Tibetan landscape. This short paper continues along that theme, with some updated statistics and information regarding China's continued oppression of this once iconic land. Satellite photos illustrate the negative impact on Larung Gar and the eviction of monks and nuns due to what Chinese authorities feel is overcrowding. Can Tibet count on the international community to bring relief to its culture and way of life, seems idealistic, because as Richard Bush III from Brookings told me in 2009, the international community recognizes Tibet as part of China. Some nation-states have sown their seeds of labour discord by incorporating a percentage of their economy toward inexpensive Chinese imports. Chinese labour standards and fierce competition make it very hard to walk away from a good deal or attempt to attach conditions that link human rights to trade. The strength of China can be seen as it develops a "vice-like grip" on the Spratley Islands, while its neighbours look to the international community to support the UN Tribunal's decision at The Hague in 2016. Despite Chinese subsidies, the central government in Beijing continues to mollify some Tibetans with labour to modernize their homeland. Sadly, though, these Tibetan's are being left behind by Chinese immigrants emboldened by a reformed hukou system dominated by Mandarin speaking, Han Chinese émigrés. Xi Jinping's hardline approach to managing the graft, and "One Belt, One Road" initiative stands to create the nexus of a bipolar world with a China- U.S. economic heavyweight tilt. Tibetan culture, land and the environment are the resultant "urbancide" as coined by Rinzin Dorjee.

Table of Contents

Introduction

Xi Jinping assumed the office of China's Presidency in 2012. He has consolidated the role of military commander and Party leader during his time as President, which has not been seen since the period of Mao Zedong, and has elevated Xi's influence with the indoctrination of "Xi Jinping Thought on Socialism with Chinese Characteristics for a New Era" during the recent 19th National Congress. Xi has made reducing the graft his primary policy plank in his first term and is now set to build his legacy in his second term. Those policies that are prominent focus on creating a stronger military, taking a more noticeable role in international affairs, while fostering China's interest in the Belt & Road Initiative (OBOR) with the goal of linking China with Europe through Asia and the Near East. Although impressive in scope, the essence is of China's domination in economic matters in the East that will cement their status as the global economic engine. The Peoples Republic of China and public sector SOE's (State Owned Enterprises) have been duly criticized for corruption since the dawn of China as a nation-state, though, the graft has been most recognizable since Deng Xiaoping opened up the economy following the crisis at Tiananmen Square, and is evident since the early days of Confucianism.[1]

---

[1] Lieberhal. Kenneth. The Legacies of Imperial China. p.4
Lieberthal indicates that Deng's moves towards tax reforms following Mao's death were constrained by the need to collaborate with local officials, while securing their loyalty. The sheer size of the Chinese bureaucracy bestowed upon its leaders a chaotic means of trusting public officials to adhere to openness and honesty within the government rank and file.

This opportunity has provided Xi with the authority to reduce the graft among the public and private spheres within China, stem the flow of investment through the Diaspora that seek to leave mainland China to embrace a freer, more palpable form of democracy, while cracking down on dissident provinces such as Uighur, Xinjiang, and Tibet, that give rise to periods of unrest, given provocation by concerned Chinese officials. For this paper, the focus will be on Tibet's historical claims to independence and the narrative of China's occupation since 1949, the impact of China's decision to militarize the Spratley Islands archipelago, and Tibet's pursuit of democracy including protection of culture, religious traditions, and the status of Tibetan refugees. President Xi's monopolization on power has seen China's foreign policy remain steadfastly pro trade, expansion of the military, with an eye toward reunifying Taiwan with Mainland China. Militarization of The Spratly Islands that lie within The South China Sea, and control approximately 1/3 rd. of the world's shipments for trade provide additional trade influence in the region, and security. [2]Xi, however, as his predecessors, remains committed to a rigid Tibetan policy, while ratcheting up the spectre of colonial pursuits to broaden China's hold in Asia. The United Nations Arbitral Tribunal ruled against China in 2016 setting off negotiations between those nation-states that were seeking recourse from China, while sowing the seeds for militarization among those nation states opposing China which comprise Southeast Asia.

---

[2] Reuters has reported on February 25, 2018 that the CCP has introduced an amendment that would allow Xi to stay in office, indefinitely.

A Historical Narrative on Tibet

Tibet was formed as a continent that evolved from an underwater vestige of mountains and land as part of India that impacted with Asia approximately forty million years ago. Indeed, the Himalayas were formed as a result of this tectonic shift.[3] Given the high altitude in Tibet, the region remains inhospitable to migrants not accustomed to the lifestyle that is necessary to survive. Moreover, the delicate nature of its ecosystem requires that care of, and concern for the environment, is paramount to maintaining the environment for future generations. Historically, Tibet belonged to a feudal system that placed an economic burden on the monastic system to appropriate wealth in a "trickle down" effect from the top that included The Dalai Lama and other religious figures. The mainstay of the economy depends upon agriculture, livestock, mining, construction and the Buddhist Monastic community and economy (which is fallen victim to urbancide and downsizing.)

The Sinicisation of the Himalaya's

Tibet is considered nor an enemy of the state or friend of the state ("Guójiā de péngyǒu",) only a component of the mainland with many economic tentacles to manoeuvre around its neighbours, such as India, for financial gain.
It is an autonomous region in principle that requires subsidies from the central government to maintain its position as another gear for the Chinese economy.

---

[3] Powers, John. Introduction to Tibetan Buddhism. New York: Snow Lion, 2007.

Since Edmund Hillary and Tenzin Norgay conquered Mount Everest in 1953, the commercialization of The Himalayas has created a "cottage-industry" inside Tibet regarding tourism that has galvanized Beijing toward claiming the Tibetan Autonomous Region for urbanisation and as another province in their federal tiara. The surge towards modernization led to The Dalai Lama fleeing Tibet in 1959 in the aftermath of a failed uprising against China, whose administration had arrived with the promise of fairness in religious and political matters, only to slowly grind out a place for socialism that was brutish and extremely damaging to the Tibetan people and their religious heritage. Damaged or destroyed were countless religious artifacts, monasteries, and the deaths of innocent people, not including those affected during Mao's failed collectivization policy from 1958-1961. The Panchen Lama, the 2nd most powerful authority during Tibet's feudal era, maintained some semblance of credibility within Tibet's leadership and among the administration of the PRC. He drafted and submitted a petition to Chinese Premier Zhou Enlai in 1962 indicating the transgressions against Tibetans since the failed uprising and The Dalai Lama's exile in India. The document: "70,000 Character Petition" illustrated eight points that the Panchen Lama felt were inhibiting Tibetans in their daily lives. Among his concerns were severe suppression against those involved in the 1959 uprising, including improper confiscation of property, food shortages that were created by Chinese officials who overstated production levels for their gain, (that saw Tibetan agriculture subsidizing China during the 'Great Leap Forward') and Tibetans that were arrested en masse after the 1959 uprising and were imprisoned without trial or proof of guilt, that affected 10-15% of the population. In addition, people died in labour camps and were summarily executed by opposing Chinese authorities; cadres destroyed shrines, sutras and Buddhist artifacts; and finally, Buddhist traditions and religion were suppressed in order to better assimilate Han Chinese that were emigrating from their homeland in a cultural engineering "tour de force" by Chinese officials.[4] Despite the status quo in Tibet that reflects a nomadic and holistic lifestyle, Beijing has to wrestle with an ever-growing population that has exceeded 1,383,767, 567 as of 2018.[5] Chinese authorities contend that Tibet offers much promise for development from a raw resource-rich province into a sprawling urban centre to expand China's monetary, and ultimately, its colonial pursuits in Asia.

Chinese leaders have been touting the miracle of the Tibetan economy, since the occupation. Bloomberg Business Week reported recently that Tibet's economy had outperformed China's on a regular basis at a rate of 12.4% compared to the rest of China at a rate of 10%. There is one notable caveat: subsidies. Since the occupation, China has invested 100 billion in the region, including infrastructure such as the Qinghai-Tibet railway linking the capital Lhasa with the mainland at Xining, Qinghai Province.[6] At it highest peak, this railway travels at 16,640 feet above sea level, which demonstrates Beijing's technological prowess that validates Beijing's interest

---

[4] Kieswetter, Kevin. Chariots of Fire: A Tibetan Historical Perspective. CreateSpace. 2014. 20. 21.

[5] "Population of China (2018.)" Population of the world. 2018. 29 January 2018. https://www.livepopulation.com/country/china.html>. For a detailed current update of Chinese demographics, this site provides a live figure and as breakdown by religious and ethnic groups.

[6] Roberts, Dexter. "Tibet Can't Kick Its Subsidy Habit." 16 December 2015.Bloomberg BusinessWeek. 19 March 2016. <http://www.bloomberg.com/news/articles/2015-12-17/tibet-spotemkin-

in changing the technological nature of the Tibetan landscape. As NASA is to America, the technocratic zeal at the Ministry of Science and Technology aptly showcases Chinese fortitude in Research & Development. Ironically, according to his biography, Dr.Wan Gang, who leads this department is not a Communist Party member and a PRC loyalist- must consider political aims first and environmental issues alternatively, without the threat of voter reprisal. Thus, the intent to transform Tibet from an agrarian feudal economy into a modern command economy is fraught with a high-risk high-reward outcome for Chinese authorities who face the wrath of established Tibetan's and the international community for human rights abuses and environmental degradation. Now, the "factory of the world" is winning this political contest. History is on the cosmological side of spiritual-Tibet; the international community supports the hegemonic economic ideals of the central government through trade agreements such as TPP (Trans Pacific Partnership), which Canada has ratified in January 2018. To this point in time, Beijing has engulfed itself in a monologue that ends with the sovereign state of China encompassing Tibet, Taiwan, The South China Sea, and the quasi-democratic city-state of Hong Kong. However, as China aligns itself with Russia whom it is relying on for energy (and sovereign democracies for exports,), it risks alienating rank and file members of economic unions over currency caps and mistrust concerning environmental concerns that threaten the airway and hydrologic cycles of the Eastern hemisphere.

---

economy>.

Indeed, the vanguard of cap and trade carbon taxation aims squarely at those nation-states that emit the highest levels of co2. The top three polluters are China, the United States, and India. Some of the current members of the international community that have a carbon tax for co2 emissions include Ireland, Sweden and a failed attempt by Australia. However, Xi Jinping, in a game of brinksmanship with the U.S. has a carbon tax planned for 2020. The tax is a starting point at the regional level with the idea to nationalise the scheme beginning with power plants. Potential problems include the administration of such a program, the technical limitations of companies to adopt the scientific means to adapt their industries and monitor emissions, not to mention the necessary judicial wrangling that will be required to bring all of the provinces on board.[7] While the two economic powers jostle over trade agreements, currency valuation, and human rights issues, the situation in the South China Sea over shipping lanes and militarization on a patch of reefs in The Spratley Islands has created a "source de préoccupation" in the international community. Vietnam, The Philippines, Taiwan, Malaysia and Brunei have competing claims to these shipping lanes that might be rich in oil and gas deposits that have the potential to exacerbate further any goodwill that exists between these long-time neighbours and prudential partners in the region. Suffice it to say, any threat of military escalation harkens back to the Suez Canal dispute, which resulted in

---

[7] Hongliang, Chai. "Carbon Trading in China Unlikely To Go National By 2017." 12 January 2016. chinadialogue.net. 22 March 2016. To be fair, nation-states such as Canada are facing the same difficulties imposing a carbon tax that is fair and responsible. In Ontario, the provincial government has cut the emission-testing fee for automobiles to curry favour to the electorate and prepare them, at least, intellectually, for a new tax.
<https://www.chinadialogue.net/blog/8538-Carbon-trading-in-China-unlikely-to-go-national-by-2-17/en>.

Egyptian President Gamal Nasser nationalising the Canal and the ouster of colonial powers, Britain and France from plundering control of the trade region in the Near East. Indeed, the loss of these two allies in the region shifted power to an ever-growing America influence in global affairs post World War II. China is, in effect moving towards nationalising the South China Sea shipping lanes and surrounding islets by asking for an IATA flight code to monitor flights in the area and permit their permission when approaching the region. America is baulking at such a request because some of these reefs have been artificially constructed and have not naturally occurred. As mentioned, the UN Tribunal has ruled against China, thus, throwing the region into a quest for militarising lands that these nation-states value for strategic, security, and economic purposes. For the record, UNCLOS (United Nations Convention Law of the Sea) became effective in 1994. The provisions include state sovereignty over waters 12 miles from the shoreline while allowing for the right of transport through international waters.[8]

Legislation reached through diplomacy for the importance of the present time and prospects of The South China Sea gives future generations of Chinese citizens and their neighbours a modus operandi for trade agreements and a stronger case for citizenship, without threat from neighbours that possess formidable military means, economic wherewithal within the international community, and the political

---

[8] Karns, Margaret P and Karen A. Mingst. International Organizations. Boulder: Ruienner, 2004. The agreement gives coastal states the right to "explore, exploit, conserve and manage natural resources" from 200 miles from baseline. Because of competing claims by China's neighbours, the overlapping of legal boundaries promises to provide new legislation that limits all parties in their quest to manipulate movement in the South China Sea. Perhaps China has the most to lose by assuming victory, while others may find the status quo requiring more management costs to police and navigate their territorial waters driving up the price of goods.

infrastructure to contain adversaries that may be plotting against it. The South

China Sea entanglement needs to incorporate balance between America co-opting

China's neighbours in the region and China simultaneously expanding its presence

through militarisation on the Spratley reefs, according to scholars versed on the

situation.[9] Despite the sense of calm advocated by America, China is displaying

through its various spokespeople a form of rhetoric that is typical of Cold War

adversaries and not the two most influential economic global powers. In the event of

hostilities, diplomacy should prevail because China, while growing stronger

militarily, is short on the necessary ingredients of war to succeed in a confrontation

in the Pacific Rim, whose nation-states align ideologically with America. Philippine

President Rodrigo Duterte, who has garnered a reputation for extra-judicial killings

of drug offenders, has cordial relations with Beijing despite the Philippines as a

claimant to the UN Tribunal. Regarding Taiwan, the question of loyalty to China

remains split towards American sales of munitions (1.83 bn) to support it

from Chinese aggression and Taiwanese sovereignty, and Taiwanese trade with

China that comprises 20% of Taiwan's total exports (though exports to China in

2015 tumbled 12.3% because of the sluggish Chinese economy.)[10] While both

countries are co-dependent on each other for commerce, the issue of trade and

politics in the Spratley's continues a historical pattern dating back to 1949 when

---

[9] Rapp-Hooper, Mira. "China's Short-Term Victory In the South China Sea." Foreign Affairs
March 2016. 25 March 2016. <https://www.foreignaffairs.com/articles/china/2016-03-
21/chinasshort-term-victory-south-china-sea.> The author gives reverence to Kenneth Waltz and
Stephen Walt regarding their commitment to multi-lateralism as a means towards solving political
impasses through diplomacy.
[10] Faith Hung & Roger Tung. "UPDATE 1 - Taiwan Dec exports fall again, economy seen
staying in recession." Reuters. 8 January 2016. 3 April 2016.
<http://www.reuters.com/article/taiwaneconomy-exports-idUSL3N14Q3S920160108>.

Chiang Kai-Shek's fledgling Nationalist Party fled China for Taiwan in the aftermath of Mao's successful communist movement in China. The U.S. formally recognized the Chinese communist government in 1979, despite U.S. President Richard Nixon's rapprochement policy that helped to pave the way for diplomatic relations between China and America in 1971. [11] The U.S. trade deficit with China was 347 billion (U.S. exports were 169.3 billion; Chinese imports were 478.9 billion) in 2016 according to the 'Office of the United States Trade Representative' a figure and amount that is perplexing to American Presidents who, like Donald Trump, seek a "Made in America" plank to foster jobs for its economy.[12] Taiwan has agreed to purchase 1.4 bn in arms from the U.S. with President Trump's authorisation, much to the protests of Chinese officials. It is, after all a business deal with a small country that is vying for protection in the region. Could arms sales of this magnitude be considered "Hard-Power"? Perhaps, an argument can be made if the purchaser would use these arms recklessly. However, movement of arms of this magnitude suggests a 21st c proxy war between America and China with what appears to be North Korea holding the balance of power in the region at the dismay of the Trump Administration. An argument can be made for an arms depot where large arms purchases must pass with UN approval to circumvent "black-market" trade that undermines democracy in nation-states, such as the annexation of Crimea by Russia in March 2014. Currently, U.N. Sanctions have had the desired effect of improving

---

[11] Michael Roberge and Youkyung Lee. "China-Taiwan Relations." Council on Foreign Relations. 11 August 2009. 3 April 2016. <http://www.cfr.org/china/china-taiwanrelations/p9223>.

[12] Office of the United States Trade Representative. "U.S. – China Trade Facts." 30 January 2018. < https://ustr.gov/countries-regions/china-mongolia-taiwan/peoples-republic-china>.

relations between the two Koreas. North Korea would like America to call their troops home with an eye towards reunification of the Korean peninsula. North Korea is lacking in authenticity and allies, whereas the South with the benefits of democracy can manage the prospect of reunification with American allies on economic and migration issues.

"Soft-power" as Joseph Nye conceived of in 1990, is a more sensible approach to American foreign policy than military aggression in the aftermath of the failed "shuttle diplomacy," that has been the hallmark of the developed world since WWII. Some scholars might argue that American hegemony is attributed to the rise in Islamic fundamentalism because of its support of Israel. After the fall of the Soviet Union and the advent of softer borders, nation – states are coming to terms with those groups that are a threat to democracy. Unemployment in the developing world has led to unrest and is a catalyst for Islamic fundamentalist groups such as Islamic State seeking members to fuel their cause and provide a voice. The difficulty is balancing the need to assimilate immigration policies that are fair and sympathetic to the historical values that our founding mothers and fathers worked hard for and fought for to resolve land boundaries and galvanise political and cultural relationships that will stand the test of time, though, be amenable to cultural modifications. Hence, there is a strong need to balance American foreign policy in Asia with a healthy dose of diplomacy. America is exercising their right with their presence in Southeast Asia and the Sino maritime region to protect its interests and champion the right of the international community to utilise international waters (for trade or pleasure.) As China and Russia gain strength, the opportunities for a maritime or aviation mishap have increased. Russia is notable

for intercepting American reconnaissance flights that recently are becoming more

daring and risk-averse.

Historically, Japan and China have endured wars dating back to "The First Sino-

Japanese War" from 1894-95. In 2016, Japan installed radar on Yonaguni Island 90

miles south of Diaoyu islands that lie in contested waters in the East China Sea,

angering Chinese officials who feel this is an intrusion on Chinese sovereignty. Thus,

this endeavour will provide Japan with a constant source of data mining and

security that is having a congealing effect on China's neighbours in the region as a

result of Sino aggression.[13]

Mao wrote in 1935, a quote that may be considered the pretext of the constitution of

Communist China: "War, that monster of human fratricide, will inevitably be wiped

out by man's social progress and this will come about in the near future. But there is

only one way to do it – war against war."[14] The Maoist foreign policy was centred on

socialist states such as the USSR, which gave China and Mao, credibility and vigour.

Naturally, China was opposed to Western nation-states on ideological grounds and

its overt preference for colonialist western nation-states. Indeed, China fought the

---

[13] Nye, Joseph. "U.S. Foreign Policy in 2016 and Beyond." Horizons Discussion. Belgrade. 28 February 2016. 29 March 2016. <https://www.youtube.com/watch?v=t9WMI7kgzW0>.
Nye indicates that Chinese aggression has created a natural balance of power among China's neighbours with the Philippines welcoming U.S. power back after a long hiatus. U.S. policy has been ambivalent towards China since the 1990's supporting China's admission to the W.T.O. balanced with the U.S.-Japan security treaty i.e. Japan pays for 50,000 American troops to proffer peace. Nye refers to U.S. policy as a rebalancing towards Asia and not a pivot away from Europe.
[14] Mao (as cited in Walz, 2001, p.112) advised that "these could easily be the words of a Western Liberal; instead they are the words of an Eastern Communist, Mao Tse-tung."
Walz, Kenneth N. man the state and war. New York: Columbia University Press. 2001.

U.S. in proxy wars with Vietnam and Korea that were influenced by then Chinese Foreign Minister, Zhou Enlai. Since an Armistice was signed in 1953 to end the Korean War, North Korea still remains technically at war with South Korea, with the North prone to periods of contempt for U.S.-South Korea military exercises, displayed through missile launches. As has been the case with the Kim family, these missile launches coincide with bouts of famine and/or sanctions levied against the North for nuclear activity. Recent sanctions appear to be having positive results, though, reports indicate that North Korea is obtaining fuel through Russia who also have sanctions against them from the annexation of Crimea. Scholars can echo the sentiments of Professor Nye regarding soft power, though, with military troops inside South Korea and UN sanctions against the North Korean administration, the notion of soft-power may be a bit misleading in this case. To elucidate his opinion on the current situation in the South China Sea, Professor Nye, in a recent forum on U.S. foreign policy noted that fear exists in the international community when a country rises quickly, which can lead to uncertainty, "miscalculations and war." Further, Nye states that managing China's growing economic stature will be a focal point of this century. Tibetans must feel that a failure of diplomacy has evaded them since the Chinese occupation in 1951 under the auspices of "soft -power" within the framework of the "Seventeen Point Agreement." Details of the accord enabled language towards Chinese interference in Tibetan affairs, while simultaneously giving the purview that the then current Tibetan political system, religious customs, and status of The Dalai Lama, were sufficient. The fact remains, however, that the 7th Point is clear about the protection of lama monasteries being maintained. China's position in Tibet during the 1950's moved away from an occupier who was slowly altering the cultural and political landscape to an aggressive occupier that resulted in the seizure of "the estates of the religious and secular elites", and the shuttering of "several thousand monasteries" while installing a Communist political system. Those monasteries that were most influential in the 1959 uprising were affected at once, while many of the monks were sent to work-units or home. Some of the monasteries that were not involved in the uprising continued to function including, Tashilunpo, the "chair" of the Panchen Lama. The primary loss of artifacts and destruction took place during the Cultural Revolution a few years after the 1959 uprising.[15] There are economic opportunities that continue developing in Asia with a population base of 4,426, 683,000, according to World Population Statistics [16], that provide strength to China's exports and employment, though that growth may be hindering American development of its own economy with outsourcing of labour that has some politicians, including current U.S. President Donald Trump questioning its past foreign policy initiatives with China. In fact, Trump is trying to link a triad of American, Chinese, and North Korean diplomacy with trade between the two economic powers. Suffice it to say, China's appetitive for developing its economy and infrastructure remains co-dependent on American purchases of inexpensive Chinese goods, which augments the harsh Tibet policy of Beijing (to develop and contain those provinces that demonstrate any notion of separation or ill- will towards China) despite the subsidies that the central government is providing for those regions.

---

[15] Goldstein, Melvyn. The Snow Lion And The Dragon. Berkeley: University of California Press. 1997.
[16] "Population of Asia 2016." World Population Statistics. 1 January 2016. 26 March 2016. <http://www.worldpopulationstatistics.com/population-of-asia/>.

Separatist Notions

The separatist threat was formed during the period following China's occupation of Tibet, currently exists in Hong Kong, and periodically in Taiwan as Beijing tries to bring Taipei back under its control. The notion of human rights has been the clarion call of western nation-states dating to the Cold War; many remember the ravages of HIV/AIDS in Romania during the Ceausescu period and the focus on Africa and HIV management. How best to measure human rights in a conciliatory tone (especially those individuals who are stateless (Syria) or living in a failed- state (Somalia, Libya) versus the costs of an intervention is a problem that foreign ministers find vexing on a continual basis. Before the League of Nations, the concern for human rights was endogenous, and that would seem fanciful given the propensity of civil war to settle land claims among first world actors. However, considering that North America, Europe and the duality of Asian politics, China and her neighbours maintain a structural - peace between states despite questionable human rights practises.[17] The conquest of Russia is incorporating neo-colonial tactics at home; the scourge of China towards creating fissures among allies in the region and operating independently from international criticism is born out of the business of exports,

---

[17] Cornell Law School. "Death Penalty Worldwide." 14 April 2014. 27 April 2016. <https://www.deathpenaltyworldwide.org/country-search-post.cfm?country=China>. China executes more people than the rest of the world combined. China and Vietnam consider capital punishment a state secret, while China may feel a political backlash from the international community if actual figures were disclosed, leading to a loss of export and trade or U.N. sanctions. China and Japan, for instance, have fought brutal wars (1894-1895) & (1937-1945) and maintain embassies inside their respective country's. Moreover, China's neighbour's cite few executions compared to mainland China, where Amnesty International reported 1,000 executions in 2015.

and state - building. The UN adopted the UDHR (Universal Declaration of Human Rights) in 1948 which China and Russia are signatories. Due to the reliance on inexpensive Chinese goods to bolster western- based economies, and China's membership in the WTO (World Trade Organisation) in 2001, how can the international community in any meaningful way say no to Chinese imports that provide citizens a discount on domestic goods. Furthermore, if there are real concerns for human rights in any region, the responsibility lay with members of the international community, particularly those United Nation members who support collective-security in a serious fashion, and can offer opportunities to advance human rights with economic measures that enhance those possibilities to procure human rights in a legitimate and long-term manner. Currently, UN& U.S. sanctions are hurting FDI (Foreign Direct Investment) in Russia, however, rising energy costs that are supported by Moscow's energy policy with OPEC are bearing fruit for the Russian Republic. China, as the factory of the world, seems to get off "scot-free"as it forcefully pushes their way through the Spratley's and, distressingly, within its borders to contain Tibet, Uighur's, and Xinjiang provinces from discord with the central government. Canadian Prime Minister Justin Trudeau was in Beijing for free trade talks in the first week of December 2017, hoping to influence Chinese towards "Canadian style labour and environmental standards and gender rights" according to the Globe and Mail, with no breakthrough on this trip. In part, China is a global leader with an elaborate workforce of 806,498,521 compared to India at 496,960,163, second overall, according to World Bank estimates. [18] Indeed, since

---

[18] The World Bank. "Data: Labour Force Total." 2011-2015 estimates. 22 April 2016.

China's inception into the WTO (World Trade Organization), and the plan to embrace fiscal reforms laid out by Deng Xiaoping, annual growth has outpaced the developed world and represents 16.70%of the global economy. [19] However, without labour unions to support workers, without transparency in the justice system, democratic reforms are an ideal for those who are affected outside of the circle of SOE's and organised labour. Therein lies one of the paradoxes within the Chinese political orbit; Xi's railing against the graft is demonstrating a China that is more responsible at the government level, yet regulatory standards for industries that run afoul of the benchmarks associated with fair employment practices have some overdue modifications to align with developed world criterion. President Xi's modus operandi is to clean up the graft and corruption among China's elites and the Diaspora. The hope is for a trickledown effect to spur confidence in the management of the economy, provide stimulus for China's wealthiest to stay and invest in the homeland, while minimising the brain- drain to the west. Any and all of these factors affect the political and economic climate in restive Chinese provinces, along with the surge in jihad that is placating that core of the Muslim population on an international scale; particularly Xinjiang who face a similar dilemma to ethnic Tibetans. This is the "ruo hua" or weakness in China's social fabric that may spur change within those regions affected by separatist notions (diversification of China's ethnic makeup is affecting the balance of power.)

<http://data.worldbank.org/indicator/SL.TLF.TOTL.IN>.
[19] Trading Economics. "China GDP." 2016. 22 April 2016.
<http://www.tradingeconomics.com/china/gdp>.

In 2016, the aboriginal community of Attawapiskat in the James Bay region of Northern Ontario, Canada had experienced mass suicide attempts among the younger demographics. Various levels of government have given money and training to the community to enable them to manage mental health issues and provide a basic level of subsistence. Much of the problems for these inhabitants lay in the erosion of their aboriginal identity as their lifestyle has evolved from a male-dominated hunter and provider for the family, to an adolescent that cannot find work or purpose. In fact, women hold the few jobs available and provide the hub of support to the family and the community. Previous research by attending psychologists found that treating mental health issues was difficult because therapy was achieved through healing circles and not administered through conventional medical channels, as is the case in the developed world.[20] The problems remain the same for Canadian Aboriginals; Canada is throwing money at the Aboriginal problem without dealing with the central issue; little to no employment. For native Tibetans, the situation mirrors the helplessness of the Aboriginals, excepting that their Chinese occupiers have put severe restrictions on their culture and spiritual well being. Comparatively, the international community may observe oppression in Tibet, is aware of self- immolations by native Tibetans yet distances themselves from applying pressure on the central government due to China's economic influence and recent military expansion in Asia and burgeoning military capability. Moreover, the mass exodus of Syrians due to conflict by the Assad government, Daesh, and competing factions, demonstrates the culpability of western nation-

---

[20] Kay, Jonathan. "Moving is the only hope for communities like Attawapiskat." National Post. 16 April 2016. 19 April 2016.

states when an issue is in the vanguard of its political realm. The question for Tibetan's is how to thrust the seriousness of their situation into the forefront of western thought, as was the case with the Syrian refugee crisis. Moreover, in a general sense, is the notion of human rights a subjective right when other rights are considered - such as equality of wages, equal employment opportunities, and freedom of speech, expression, and assembly. It would seem unequivocal when contrasting judicial systems and cultures, that, yes- rights are subjective, but, basic fundamental rights should be universal no matter First, Second, Third or Fourth World (referring to Aboriginal including native Tibetans.) Once again, scholars can point to the Canadian aboriginal community as having more freedom spiritually, which is true compared to Tibetans. Both groups are in dire situations; both groups receive subsidies from the central government. Canadian aboriginals receive piecemeal support from the provincial and federal governments; Tibetans are the minority among a burgeoning Han Chinese base that is entitled to government contracts, government positions, and academic placement within government educational institutions. In addition, the cultural tradition of the Tibetan language is being minimised by Mandarin, limiting opportunities for those Tibetans who are unable to adapt or refuse to accept the lingua franca that has become the standard in the larger urban centres. Human rights have evolved and will continue to adapt as globalisation continues to strengthen its hold on the monetary system, borders remain soft, and multiculturalism is steadfast in western democracies. Keynesian economic policies are utilised in China to manage growth and guide the central bank as is common in established democracies. In this regard, China is democratising, though; the central government is slow rehabilitating human rights through the

judiciary.

The End of the One Child Policy

Garrett Hardin wrote in 1968 about the toll that humankind places onto itself by

taking more resources out of the Earth than it is returning. "The essence is that

over-population results in scarcity for each as resources become further strained. It

is fair to say that most people who despair over the population problem are trying

to find a way to avoid the evils of overpopulation without relinquishing any of the

privileges they now enjoy. They think that farming the seas or developing new

strains of wheat will solve the problem—technologically."[21]

China began to put constraints on its population with the implementation of a one

child per family policy between 1979 and 2015. The policy had an effect on the

population growth, though, it reinforced state-sponsored socialist ideology for

economic purposes. This convention was magnified through forced abortions and

limits on family size. Corruption found its way into this area of state apparatus

where public officials could be bribed to allow a couple to have more than

one child. "Social fostering fees" provided public officials with approximately two

trillion Yuan (over 300 billion USD) since the policy was adopted, according to He

---

[21] Hardin, Garrett. "The Tragedy of the Commons." SCIENCE. 13 December 1968.
www.sciencemag.org. Columbia edu courses. 30 April 2016.
<http://eesc.columbia.edu/courses/v1003/lectures/population/Tragedy%20of%20the%20Commo
ns.pdf>.

Yafu, a demographics maven who was a critic of the policy. Scholars can point to
Hardin's theory as the antecedent to China's one-child policy and possibly a
contributing influence on the central government.[22] The aftermath of The Great
Leap Forward indicates that over 55 million Chinese lost their lives during this
period. The central government and Mao were trying to regain credibility and
control of the population despite the loss of lives, while The Cultural Revolution
from 1966- 1976 created that fervor that Mao desired to create "urbancide" within
China.

There had been incidents of forced euthanasia of fetuses belonging to women that
exceeded the one-child limit. That act underlies the depth on China's human rights
decree against their citizens, that in response to one particular forced abortion of
23-year-old, Feng Jianmei set social media ablaze. The Economist quoted statistics
on child abortions at 14 million in 1983; in 2009, 6 million. Reliable figures from the
central government are not available, though; suffice it to say public officials
enforced many abortions.[23] Ms Feng's harrowing experience and public knowledge
led to an outcry against authorities that belaboured them, in part, at least to amend
the one-child policy in January 2016. The new policy applies to married couples,
only, and allows married couples to have two children. The impetus for China's
change of direction is predominantly monetary. The population is ageing and
industry will require a new generation of workers to maintain economic expansion,

---

[22] Moore, Malcolm. "Chinese couple pays L130, 000 to have a second child to avoid one-child
policy." The Telegraph. 1 June 2012. 1 May 2016.
<http://www.telegraph.co.uk/news/9305700/Chinese-couple-pay-130000-to-have-a-secondchild-
to-avoid-one-child-policy.html>.
[23] "The One-Child Policy: the brutal truth." The Economist. 23 June 2012. 1 May 2016.
<http://www.economist.com/node/21557369>.

and power the military through enlistment and education. Moreover, fetal rights in Tibet and Xinjiang provinces remain unchanged. Thus, the notion of a woman's right over the control of her reproductive system remains under state control with jurisdiction in those restive areas that the state feels threatened by separatist forces. There are reports that China's fertility police are more vociferous since the end of the one child per family policy. In a recent article, the stipulations allow couples to have a second child four years after the birth of their first, while the Planned Birth Policy forbids out of wedlock births and childbearing without authorisation even if it is the couples first child. Those females that violate these laws are being pursued by public officials, located, face abortion of the fetus, and sterilisation. The situation has become more tenuous for families and those with government positions that are confronted by job loss and other benefits if found to be in contravention of the new policy. Planned parenthood remains a strong source of income for the government, which for provides full time and part time public officials with salary and benefits in return for managing the planned parenthood of a group of families in a particular region as "cluster leaders".[24]

---

[24] Fong, Mei. "Sterilization, abortion, fines: How China brutally enforced its 1-child policy." <u>New York Post</u>. 03 January 2016. 31 January 2018. < https://nypost.com/2016/01/03/how-chinas-pregnancy-police-brutally-enforced-the-one-child-policy/>.

Tibet's Tectonic Culture Shift

The Tibetan diaspora has grown to approximately 130,000 across the globe, with the majority of refugees in India that remain stateless. Those Tibetans in America have become naturalized citizens and promote their identity. The notion of identity is crucial to Tibetans as they seek support for a return to their homeland hoping that Tibet will be virtuous to their spiritual, culture and future goals. The current Dalai Lama is at an advanced age, and the Chinese authorities indicate their preference to anoint a new Dalai Lama when HH Tenzin Gyatso passes away, circumventing the traditional means of locating and verifying an authentic heir to the previous Dalai Lama. The process of "recognition or recruitment of an incarnate lama" includes the awareness of signals that indicate to the new lamas devotees his or her "place and condition of the new birth." Signals can include "a dream occurring to a lamas follower" or a fondness for "religious practise or objects" or the "recognition of previously owned ritual items in their former life or people known in previous lives." [25]

Michael Buckley has witnessed the mass deforestation of Tibet where "half the forests of eastern and southern Tibet" have been eviscerated by its Chinese denizens.[26] Buckley continues: "...over 50% of Tibet's forests have disappeared since China invaded Tibet"...while "over 50 billion worth of oak, pine, larch, and

---

[25] Zivkovic, Tanya. Death and Reincarnation in Tibetan Buddhism. New York: Routledge. 2014.

[26] Buckley, Michael. Meltdown In Tibet. New York: Palgrave MacMillan. 2014. 6.

rhododendron has been logged and hauled out to mainland China." [27] Given the vast

amount of resources shipped out of Tibet as Buckley notes, consideration must be

accorded to mining and the loss of employment opportunities to native Tibetans due

to the sinicisation of Tibet since the occupation. As mentioned earlier, China has

invested 100 billion in the region through subsidies, though; it is the present

damage and long-term consequences of its actions that are difficult to calculate. As

Tibet is native to "46,000 glaciers" it has the third largest cluster of ice in the world

after the north and south poles, thereby earning the title of Third Pole.[28]

Larung Gar under siege

Larung Gar is known as the 'Tibetan City in the Sky.' Chinese workers are

systematically dismantling it since 2016 with the goal of reducing the cultural

impact of Buddhism on the Tibetan Plateau. Contrarily, Chinese officials cite

overcrowding as the reason for the evictions. In many cases, monks and nuns are

merely watching as their homes are taken down and they are evicted. Tibetan

authorities have been evicting Tibetan monks and nuns from Larung Gar, the largest

Tibetan Buddhist monetary in the world. In 2016, approximately 3,730 residents

were forced to leave, while 172 monks' and 1.328 nuns' residences were destroyed.

Chinese officials have a plan to place to house "97 Communist Party Cadres, who are

---

[27] Buckley, Michael. 6. China has monopolized Tibet's forestry to manufacture furniture and help supply its construction and manufacturing interests.
[28] Sangay, Lobsang. "Tibet's plea: fix the roof of the world before its too late." the guardian. 11 November 2015. 10 April 2016.
<http://www.theguardian.com/commentisfree/2015/nov/11/tibetclimate-change-paris-talks-dalai-lama>.

required to be atheist, in top finance, security and admission roles" according to recent Reuters article in January 2018. [29] Here are a few images of Larung Gar, one as a thriving small city; the others show satellite images of Larung Gar before and after the evictions in 2016.

[29] Shaw, Steve. "China Tears Down the Tibetan City in the Sky." The Diplomat. 03 August 2017. 14 December 2017. < https://thediplomat.com/2017/08/china-tears-down-the-tibetan-cityin-the-sky/>.

January 2016

April 2016